Household Hints for the End of Time

Ken Howe

Ken Howe

For Gilbert, Feb. 28/2002

Brick Books

National Library of Canada Cataloguing in Publication Data

Howe, Ken, 1960–
    Household hints for the end of time
Poems
ISBN 1-894078-16-0

    i. Title

PS8565.O8558H68 2001   C811'.6   C2001-900744-2
PR9199.3.H69H68 2001

We acknowledge the support of the Canada Council for the Arts
for our publishing programme. The support of the Ontario Arts
Council is also gratefully acknowledged.

Cover art: "Trees" by Otto Rogers.
The author's photograph is by Brad Martin.

This book is set in Minion, Sabon, Frutiger and Rotis.

Design and layout by Alan Siu.

Printed and bound by Sunville Printco Inc.

Brick Books
431 Boler Road, Box 20081
London, Ontario   N6K 4G6

brick.books@sympatico.ca

Household
Hints
for the
End of Time

Contents

The Ambient Geography

In the Closed Ecology of the Home

A Maid in Hell

Absent Friends

Preparatory Exercises for Valentine's Day

Fluff is the Enemy of Music

In Memoriam

Carol Loberg/Pfeiffer
1963-1988

The Ambient
Geography

Snow Epiphanies

1. Into the windblown thaw and an element
of cat (*felis domesticus*) on the wet
wind. Brown footprints and the red
and white blank steer face butcher sign
luminous as the light
declines. How
we must love this "snow" to be
cleaning up after it
over and over.

2. Brown kidney pool prints in the squashed drugstore
floormat. A man buying hairspray with nickels,
slow Parkinson's movements and the night
clumping down on both of us. Counting.
Stars, the disappointed stars
in their spiney jackets, shivering down
on the snowcapped parking range.

3. Any Canadian must have several psychologies of snow including:
the rooftop snow and snow sneaking up around the shutters, the
terraced spruce tree snow, the warm late-day-waking-up snow
pressed in a wall against the window, sun-setting-on-early-spring's-
ephemeral snow, the valley-hushed-and-white-with-snow snow, the
rubbed-into-your-burning-skin-and-dribbling-between-your-flushed-
shoulderblades-onto-the-hot-sheets snow.

4. Two identical snowflakes, unusual in my experience,
or rather, one snowflake, flutters by, but identical
to one I remember seeing in Edmonton in 1966,
in Emily Murphy Park on a March afternoon
(when I was more likely to notice that sort of thing)
as I stepped into the same river twice, once.

5. The moon pressing its crumbly face
against the amniotic membrane of the day
and from the aluminum of my shovel the sky
blue grey. What is the faint sunlight
saying to me, the wet wind high overhead,
weeds and sand on the exposed hillside, un-named
angel of annunciation among grimy roots?

Notes on the Urban Squirrel

> *"I think this squirrel was out cruising for victims*
> *and spotted Fred and Deborah on the road. . ."*
> -Patricia Cornwell: *All That Remains*

1. From the heart of the cone of shadow
the voice spoke its
staccato denunciations, enunciating
my failings, berating,
raining, like spruce needles
upon the ubiquitousness of impropriety.

Squirrel morality is reductive but most vociferous.

2. Urban squirrels are certainly not rats with fuzzy tails. Rats are
nocturnal social omnivorous with distinctive hairstyling and the
best legal advice. Contrast also the squirrel's sense of high moral
purpose with the rat's corrupt politicking—infecting the body
politic with young offensiveness and single motherness. Both rat
and squirrel can admittedly carry bubonic plague, though no one
much wants it anymore.

3. Squirrels encircle my sandwich, a rogue's gallery chain gang
            posturing in ratty punk haircuts.
Suddenly one pulls up in an out-of-province Oldsmobile,
            screwdriver in hand—he's snickering "they can't touch us
            boys, remember the sciurine offender's act, and besides,
            we're ALL underage."
One of them has his paws on my boot—"spare crumbs?" he jeers,
            and there's no mistaking the menace in his voice, "or
            wouldja rather I give ya some BUBONIC PLAGUE?"
Jeez behind every bush there's a squirrel, gnawing rat-a-tat-tat at
            what looks like a pineal gland, the social fabric, and like
            as not collecting benefits from YOUR tax dollars as well.
            (Come on, write to your M.P.—get the bastards before
            they get you.)

4. No new model of squirrel has been introduced in North
America since the old "stop-action" squirrels pioneered by
Hollywood B-movies in the fifties.

Since the public seems accustomed to these older models further refinements will probably concentrate on the technologies of production.

5. The squirrel explicated.
The squirrel vociferated.
The squirrel insisted.
"Be little." Said the squirrel.
"Be troth." Said the squirrel.
"Be labour." Said the squirrel.
"Be reft." Said the squirrel.

Squirrels eat eggs
And burros eat eggs
And little roe feed orcas
A kid'll feed orcas too
in the zoo.

6. The squirrel incarnates accumulated residue of human temporal consciousness scanning the future. Discontinuously it gnaws on discarded pine cones, apple cores, beernuts, stop-action clicking its way across gaps in our reasoning toward a hidden stash organized in patterns too complex for its own tiny brain.

Notes on Stanfield's Red, Duofold, Long Underwear

1. Somewhere, away on the fractured shores
of Peter Pond Lake,
a trapper emerging from his A-frame encased
in his Stanfield's Long Underwear, red
as the tone of the sepia and white print shows.

"It's part of his skin," say the characters in Jack London's stories,
and they have evidence.

    a) Studies have shown
    that one's longjohns continue to sweat after death
    and grow baggier down by the bottom trapdoor.

    b) Reliable witnesses report that they've seen sets
    of underwear
    walking onto the pier on Group of Seven mornings
    standing on cotton-wool legs
    to piss.

2. O the conundrum in the filling station
restrooms, mud on the floor
from the melt from the snowboots,
and the longjohns
bunched in one hand—not trusting
the trapdoor of course—
clutching the sweater in the same hand
as best as one can,
and the coat on its hook crowding the stall,
and the precarious
one-handed tearing of the toiletpaper
and eventually, the exasperated
twist for the flush lever,
hidden somewhere on the opposite side.

3. I once knew a married couple
who exchanged sets of Stanfield's Red Duofold
Long Underwear in lieu of wedding rings,
supporting Canadian industry over South African,

and when the husband was widowed, hers
watched over him from the closet ajar,
spoke to him in his dreams,
rehearsed the Epistle to the Corinthians,
bled on the hanger from its mistress' stigmata
(intensifying and liquifying in colour)
or became lonely, and descended
to cling to him in the night,
less itchy than wool and leaving no imprint.

4. An acquaintance of mine donned
Stanfield's Duofold Long Underwear (mine)
as sleeping garb during a visit years ago—Venus emerging
from the Strait of Juan de Fuca
framed in the window of my Victoria apartment,
her hips and shoulderblades outlined in cloth incarnadine,
cascade of her long form curved
like warm red marble on the submissive waves.

I hesitated to wash the thus sanctified garment
for years afterwards, cherishing its smells
and sandy hairs, until
fed up with its owner's ridiculous behaviour,
into the washing machine it plunged,
confecting several pairs of
glowing pink
        socks,
            shorts,
                and undershirts
on its way.

The Annotated Urban Magpie

1. Standing upwind of me in his
black heavymetal T-shirt, the magpie
lit a cigarette on the subway

platform, sunglasses reflecting
rainbows, smelling of ozone in unlaced

hightops. Then the train came and he was
gone, leaving only muddy tracks
in the furrowed stone.

2. Magpies are the incarnate shadow of our mutual inattention to each
other, marginalized explanations taking wing as quickly as they are
glossed over, glossolalia, their glossy wings and feathers,
hence their insatiable appetite for flesh, a congealed repository of
human identity.
"Stop—wait!" they peck into the hindquarters of the restless feral
deer—"Listen!" But it's too late to stop now of course, there's only a
glittering shadow remaining, spreading infection.

3. Condensing analogously to rain drops, out of vaporized glass from
            violent volcanic eruptions.
A vapour projected beyond Earth's atmosphere precipitates over the
            magnetic poles where energy from the Van Allen belts
            organizes it into what appear to be individuated life forms.
Its nearest terrestrial relatives the auroras borealis and australis, the
            resemblance discernible in the gleam on their feathers.

4. At sunrise, perched as closely as possible to a bedroom window, the
magpie loudly and comprehensively confesses for us the sins we plan
(unconsciously) to commit during the day. Over the years a dense and
highly elliptical code of cross-referencing has developed, incomprehensible
to human listeners.

Though at times disembodied feelings of, for example, anger, lust, or envy
may well up inside us as we lie listening.

5. A miniature tornado made of darkness
has touched down
in the vicinity of the garbage bags we
left overnight on the back step.

The sudden plunge in air pressure cut
an uneven swath through the packaged
mise en abyme of our day's routine
paying particular attention to

bloodsoaked kleenexes, raw meat,
and anything sticky. The fury of Mother Nature
operating on all levels.

Canadian Rockies Trailguide: Iceline Trail

1. *Yoho Approach*

Although ascending
the air grows damp with ferns and liverwort
skunk cabbage, dampness percolating through the wood,
a sleeping reptile faintly luminous
perhaps part of your brain
its tongue flickering through the underbrush,
the heavy scent of decomposing wildflowers.

Poplars scrape and fawn,
choking in the mottled light, drained of photons
by the upwardly mobile spruce.
The reptile, still unconscious, is the trail
holding you absently in its jaws,

> tossing its head.

"Brute, brutish, brutal"
your only recognizable thoughts—
you translate them into various languages,
none of them human, as you ascend,
the razor's edge of consciousness ground down in the
mortor and pestle of your hip joints
while your heart executes
a virtuosic *accelerando, poco a poco,*
rondo alla turca into an unsteady *trill*
fermata, always rising.

> This is eternity,
the sum total of your earthly existence sadly ascending
in arbitrary coils. You are

> stuffed in a dappled sack lifted by a crane of sunlight,
kicked randomly from all directions
by your own hiking boots, choking
on this rank and paradisical perfume.

2. *Yoho Lake Bypass*

All is open.
The monumental egotism of the waterfall, Takkakaw
pervades this gravel pit in reverse,
scrawny plume in the distance
pathetic, contemptible,
barely loud enough to drown the wind.

Not, however, the uninterrupted whine
of my quadraceps, the direct communication of
glutius patheticus singing a quavering blues.
"Gravel. Grovel. Drivel," ejects the unconscious,
apparently acclimatizing. Rhapsody
                    on a limestone quarry.
Hyperextended gravel church parking lot.

3. *Iceline*

High high high by the ice
arriving
the hiker's high defining
most of the clinically observed
variations on vertigo
        imposing
in this place
            a pause
this wrecking yard for oddsize
pyramid parts in the preserving
dull snowlight. To sleep,
                perhaps expire
never again to incline upwards
but to sink, sink, sink
into this stairwell stone,
and petrify,
        a round discordant note among the neumes
            the scattered blocks
terraced
                        earthwards.

In the Closed Ecology
of the Home

The Deconsecration of a House (in steps)

First:
Adopt the doctrine of Nestorianism—the sanctity of the home
subsumed into the quality of its immaculateness. The maintenance of
this state.

Second:
I am dimly aware of an oleaginous residue from the soles of my feet,
building up on the linoleum, diagramming a Lorenz attractor of
indiscreet points. Outside trafficked areas a paste of spilled sauces and
vegetables increases in uniformity, incubating fungi which leak slowly
into the atmosphere and are filtered by my bronchial tubes.

Third:
Inertia erases the border between
habitat and inhabitant.
The vacuum cleaner gets
heavier and heavier, its silence pressing down
upon my prostrated tympanum.

Miasms seep from its dust-crusted flue.

Fourth:
Thermal energy from
feverish dustmite activity
has created an inversion layer
above the livingroom rug. A winterkill line
has appeared in the fungus growing on the walls.

Fifth:
Lying face down on the bathroom floor, I detect peripherally a spider
wiping its feet as it steps onto its corner web. Hyperevolved dust
bunnies have left avalanche trails in the grey bathtub moraine.

Envoi:
From domicile to occupied territory,
the recurring cycle of cathexis and abandonment.

Tomatonotes

1. O tomato
        sun sponge
in the garden swelling
new-burned
            food blister

2. I was so worried about the tomatoes' risk
        of frost, the moon being so
                    close so
leaning
        toward the night of discolouration
in the so
        glacial surface
                    the face
of the paleolithic hunter preserved therein.

3. The Roman god of the tomato was Bacchus, a portfolio he
inherited through his attachment to the vine. Soft tomatoes were
hurled at him in his cart during processions.
Ovid says his mother standing by at his dismemberment was
transformed into a tomato, her tears ripening red and warm as
they flowed.

4. After placing stakes in the ground
        to restrain my movements
I slept in the garden that frosty night—
        curled around its
                curling vine.

5. *Tomatum swellum ipsum esse*,
(as they say in Thomistic philosophy)
for the swelling of the tomato is its life, therefore
(they explain) its act-of-being.

6. *Les Rois ne touchent pas aux tomates* while
Barons of Finance
never touch tomatoes.
Unschooled in direct contact with

incarnated suffering, that
skin too smooth for abstract hands,
swollen without the fissures of a lip—
the glassy place
above her hip perhaps
or reified
the parchment smoothness of a thigh.

7. Gumboot morning—the pussywillow wind
claws from spring and a low sky shivering
under its military issue wool blanket. Daylight
tramples my frost-ravaged garden—
sun beams clubbing two-by-four stilts
stumping across the ruined soil—stalks,
tubers, vines
but not the already-gathered tomato,
maringuouin gonflé, emportée
        sur une mer amère.

Inside the house, where no frost can reach,
the ripe bathtowel-foal-nose into lymph nodes
nuzzles. In the window the red
lantern of tomato globe *in situ*
sits on the sill, raised up. Glowing
master of this house—
no storm shall slit you—
Rather will you tinge the multitudinous
        stews I boil
                incarnadine.

Assorted Views of Chocolate Cake

1. There the sweet

    heart of darkness oozing

        ichor out of every pore.

Nocturnal palpitation.   Chocolate midnight.

2. And in the refrigerator one
graph-like wedge missing
from its brown circumference, the
education budget perhaps, approximately,
so that it seemed to me if I could just avoid
touching the icing, just
even out the jagged edges
the cake would remain
essentially
intact.

           And then it seemed sufficiently
           discreet, to form a slight concave
           bit by bit merely
           rounding the hidden surface inside—
           the icing still untouched

           until

     spelunking in that dark chocolate
underworld by suppertime
the ravaged ruin of hollow icing-shell
was all that there remained, brown
exoskeleton of some butter cocoa
sugar beetle long extinct washed up
on the chill beach of the fridge.

3. Getting past the cakemix was often difficult
the siren-call of the soft snow powder
gently dusting my tongue

as I drew spoonfuls from the sac
at hurried moments.

 "No time to bake anything now"
I'd say while the mix disappeared mysteriously,
gradually from the package,
sand in an hourglass.
World petroleum resources.
Forests.
  Childhood.

4. The cake squatted
like a sea-sponge sucking through my own mouth in sweet
expanding forkfilling amoebic I absorbed absorbing mouth
stretched ecstatically across the mounting mound of Earth Mama
icing effluvial.

Then the realization: Stoppage. My gag reflex stoppered velum
clogged corkfilled *you have five minutes of consciousness* work
methodically think clearly *you have five minutes of consciousness* do
not aspirate cake fragments pry with a butterknife *you have five
minutes of consciousness* work the jaw pound pound cake cakeing
pharyngeal obstructing structure.

  dark cocoa powder edges of consciousness closing on
my running eyes and nose. Darkness closing.

  And beachedfish the breathing and the slimed Duncan
Hines cast of my throat lies on the kitchen table. Sun pouring in like
oxygen through the kitchen window.

But you know cowboys, when you fall off a horse, you gotta get
right back on.

Notes on Mushrooms

1. Against the barn the mushrooms grow
wet. Brown lipstick caked on
their pouty mouths, as bi-valvular
they suck the soaked and
shredded straw.

2. Not having underarms, mushrooms cannot be persuaded to use
deodorant. They consider themselves to be the incarnation of the smell of
wet earth as it dreams of the sea. Deodorized, they would cease to exist.

3. Because it possesses consciousness, the mushroom must be classified as
animal rather than vegetable. Its smooth cortextual surface should not be
taken as indicating a lack of sophistication. Conventional measures of
animal intelligence, which calculate cerebral mass in proportion to total
body weight, show the mushroom to be fully six times as developed as
human beings.

4. Certain varieties of *Aminita* secrete casings of crystal endorphins
around irritating sediment particles which become embedded in their
surface, so as to maintain a uniform consistency of inner peace. It is to
these extremely rare "pearls of great price" that Jesus refers in Matthew
13:45.

5. The "boot" mushrooms that Alex picked turned into live slugs when
cooked, writhing in our barley soup, furred against our tongues. Then
they stained our mouths blue, like squid.

6. The moorhen shunned the moon
a darkened tomb upon the heath. Rheumatic, upon
the bleak moor where romance loomed. A
billowing futon of humus loomed upon the
mushy mossy heath, looming before her pedantic
fluids, full and round and darksmelling ground:
"I am not a mushroom," the voice protested,
"nor do I commune with these. My advocacy is
disinterested. Cold as their caress."
Milky cataracted eyes staring blankly at the sky.

7. Mushroom martyrdom. All mushrooms
are hermaphroditic, containing both testosterone
and estrogen in equal measure. Yet many varieties lactate
and one manifests a pattern of nerve endings identical
to that of the human testicle. (Specimens
should be thoroughly dried before slicing or chopping.)

8. The shyness of mushrooms is legendary—they peek in huddled
groups from under mats of wet leaves and earth, their hands clasped
tightly together. It is very rare to see them smile.

A Refrigerator

In the wintertime it is difficult not to be impressed by the redundancy of the operation: in the middle of a painstakingly heated and maintained shell of warmth, a certain rectangle of air is chosen to be recooled.[1] This is the area where time, recently, has stood still.[2] A millet pastry occupies the centre, half-eaten, framed by exotically sliced eggplant, English cucumber, and a jar of ginger marmalade. It has all been there for some weeks now yet remains as fresh, wholesome and inviting as on the day of its concoction. The milk, which in other environments would be clotted and imbued with a raw biting smell remains pure and liquid; cheeses retain their consistency and do not increase in value; expiry dates, acknowledging their new-found redundancy, have begun adjusting themselves to maintain a constant interval relative to the present. Occasionally in the night I open the door to consider this marvel. Objects attend,[3] peacefully, in the pale gleam of an automatic light bulb. If I eat something, will it break the spell?

---

[1] In the universe of this discussion though, the agent has been changed. Cold not being adequate to the task. Fluorocarbons in circulation, like lymph or stars. A stability that is not inert. Think rather of the sun arrested at its zenith, held there by GOD. Only a reification could manipulate another reification, after all.

[2] Cf. Rogers and Hart, "My Heart stood still."

[3] I have suppressed the object of the verb here, since I have no idea what these things are waiting for. Personify an object and right away it starts to wait. Pumpkins are a disconcerting example. Every year when Hallowe'en is over, pumpkins all down my street begin waiting for something until their heads cave in or passersby run up from the street and punt them across the yard. Pumpkin observers must realize (in fear and trembling of course) that this personification is their own projection, and composes very little of the pumpkin's aggregate essence.

A Window

Uncovered are eggs over the clean emulsion of watersprites and puffing snowbanks. In sudden reconstitutions of winter the window transmits objectivity, tinting the ice-clouds grey and playing subtly with their temperatures. It is the prime matter of observation, transparent like water or air but unmoving.[1] Unified by the frame. Curtained, the window is a cataract of undulating cream[2] that splashes us warmly and leads us into introspective *frames of mind*. In principle every window is, potentially at least, a universe. The problem arises when a window is manipulated, as in, the *picture window* or the *display window*.[3] These windows remain, however, scrupulously inclusive, embracing stray cats, dust, and electric cords with the same disinterested enthusiasm. Have you ever tried to walk through a window?[4]

---

[1]Not *stagnant*, but *unmoving*.

[2]This is of course a reference to Rideau Falls, which people commonly crawl in behind so they can look out at passing sailboats on the Ottawa River. Large trilobites inhabit the gallery behind the falls, which often crawl between the toes of explorers and incite attacks of anachronism.

[3]I am thinking of a certain *display window* on Queen Street East, where Christmas Music was played during the month of December and figurines of sinister elfish types with reindeer were installed under a continuous sifting of fluffy snow. For the western observer this was confusing because of the exterior temperature, which hovered nervously around fifteen degrees (see also: Emperors and Butterflies.)

[4]You too can be included by a window, but the window *scene* you saw will thereby, *ipso facto*, disappear. Or be replaced by a new window. A moving window. You will become a Canadian Pacific dome car threading its way through the Rockies. The Undersea Gardens in Victoria Harbour. You will take your clothes off and root furiously in roadside snowbanks. You will eat the soil of mountain vistas. You will tear your skin off and plunge into the salt salt sea.

A Microwave Dish

Regarding the infinitely permeable coldness of the glass, the inferiority of the human genitalia is immediately apparent. The sky canopy[1] of stretched permeability, a microcosmic surface to contain convection. Visions cookware is radically open, its abdomen of sweet potatoes and prune tsimmes pulsing like the visible man alive[2], the shy bubbles gestating and throbbing like tiny ventricles. Regarding these bubbles[3], which are the visible manifestation of emotive bilocation[4]: they demonstrate the prophetic tone of ceramic under certain conditions. Dissecting the dish afterward we find a banquet laid out for us in the flesh pinned-back, incense floating through our nostrils and lifting us two or three millimetres above the bedsheets where the brutal friction of cotton fibre cannot reach[5].

---

[1]Regarding the microwave band: theologians (that is, not *certain* theologians but *all* theologians) are aware that these microwaves are the agent of divine activity in the universe. You can, as you probably know, contemplate them directly, through your short-wave radio.

[2]The Visible Man™ (c. 1959), who nurses his young, is in this case a woman.

[3]I am tempted to include here research data on the efficacity of Coca-Cola as a spermicide. But this might not communicate my real concern, which is the spiritualization of sexuality through human transcendence. Question for discussion: what is the role of (contraceptive) technology in this development?

[4]I am sure we have all experienced this at one time or other. Bilocation of the noetic being causes a drop in internal pressure and the formation of anaximenitic bubbles in the upper respiratory tract. We know this phenomenon from "the bends," where a diver's too-quick decompression causes dissolved nitrogen to bubble up in the blood. Emotive bilocation is usually sensed as an attack of vertigo or as a "lump in the throat" during moments of intense communion.

[5]*Transubstantiation* is not the same as *change*. In any case it is music that is supposed to be the food of love. If only music would show some initiative, though. If it would wrap itself around us like a hot amoeba and choke us in oceans of apricot jello. If it would lather our bodies with bitter soap and slide us through enormous shower curtains of Easter lilies. But it rarely does. The human imagination is probably an evolutionary compensation for this failure.

A Cider Bottle

Months after the contents have been consumed there remains a shallow quagmire of juice evaporating and precipitating infinitely in the closed ecology of the bottle.[1] Floating islands of mold form and evolve in an ontogenetic replication of natural succession in terrestrial forest, driven by the changing composition of the hermetic atmosphere.[2] The development of this universe will not, however, parallel our own. Its course is controlled by the organic memory of the apple particles which predominate in the bottled community. While the inhabitants of this system will probably never resemble apples themselves, each will carry within its soul a tiny flowering tree that bears fruit every spring.[3]

[1] I hope you will not be too offended if I forbid you to think of this consumption as a negative thing. This non-alcoholic cider was drunk at joyful celebrations, on returning from parties of manual collective outdoor labour, on fresh mornings with the winter sun streaming in the windows. *Consumption* may have the same root as *consummation*.

[2] I leave out the factor of sunlight, since the bottle has been sitting near a window. But to contemplate a closed system is always to imply a horizon which one transcends through this very act of contemplation. Imagine pieces of claustro-phobic mold, trapped in bottles like Greek philosophers seeking happiness. The horizon is accessible, we tell them, only to the imagination.

[3] Some may interpret this as a reference to *aspergillis*, which under a microscope resembles a tree sprouting gleaming spheroid spores. But I am really thinking of a mythical backdrop to human experience: the story of Eve. Eve didn't eat an apple, of course, but you can. If you want to come over, I have some in my refrigerator right now.

Nothing Scary in the House

Early evening.
I come home from a tough
    game of road hockey,
the family around the T.V. set—
nothing unusual about that.

I take a chair, an easy chair, in the
    corner of the room.
I take it easy, on the chair, look at the screen—
a test pattern. An ordinary test pattern.

What's going on mum? I say
addressing my mum, meaning
the test pattern.

"Nothing unusual going on"
says my dad, answering for my mum
which is not unusual, "station problems
are only temporary." Nothing creepy at all.

I say good night and
go upstairs.
My footsteps echo in the dark hallway—
as they should.
I wash my hands, brush my teeth.
Nothing sinister about that.

I floss.

I go into my bedroom, sit
down on my bed without
looking underneath it.

And why would I look under my bed there's
nothing under my bed. Nothing
evil under my bed.
Nothing wicked or malevolent under my bed.
Nothing brooding, resentful
of human life, of happiness, of sunlight.
Nothing accursed from the dawn of time, steeped
in thousands of years of bitterness.
Nothing plotting the ruin and overthrow of
joy, goodness, or innocence.
Nothing grasping or malicious.
Nothing with long sharp teeth or green glowing eyes,
grasping with bony fingers
at the ankles of children who rise
tremblingly in the darkness,
driven by an irresistible call of nature
into the clutches of a nocturnal fiend that feeds
on fear and puerile flesh, sucking
the soul like marrow from the bone, no
demon from the vilest pits of

Hell no,
there is nothing anything like that under my bed.

Nothing scary in the house.

A Maid in Hell

¡Hola Chele! A Voyage South

In the distant *norte* of *Norte America*
While fluffy December shifts into January
    windows have been shut tight.
The consumption of hot chocolate and marshmallows has
skyrocketed.
    Orion twinkles through a haze of halogen interference.

Triton, moon of water, supports life in thermal currents
    under the ice. Honduras
    under the crushing bulk of North America
    also remains fluid.

With a lifeline of American dollars, I

                         plunge.
January thaw will be particularly violent this year.

    Brown water, splashing.
    Thick hands pounding
    clothes against a stone. Bare
    breasts. Ferns and a dress
    spread upon the bank.
    Amid the rocks naked children frolic.

I have landed in a copy of *National Geographic*.

        El Progreso: Nine o'clock. Eighty
        thousand people invisible as we ride
        into town in the truck of the *Colegio*
        San José. A fluorescent light reveals
        shadows, ghosts, shapes of chickens.
        A road of sand. One headlight. Huge
        flickering leaves.

The sun has risen the hills
overgrown compost heaps of tangled green.
Crayola emerald. Arboreal Oz. Spread
lush life of leaves tumble. Clouds
precipitate out of the liquid air, sky

golden blue.
A loudspeaker on an invisible white van
blasts: *"¡Digestivo, antiacido, refrescante estomacál!"*
On the bedpost a cockroach the size of my fist
eyes me suspiciously.

> "But how can we have the *gringo* in
> our group if he doesn't even know
> how to speak? What will he do?"
> they ask Sister *Carmen* in Spanish. I
> speak. "He sounds almost as if he
> knew what he was saying," they tell
> each other.

> A priest gives me a ride to a village
> near the *aldea* where I will live. I ride
> in a truck box overgrown with
> teenagers. Try to remember their
> names. Fail. A girl named *Daisy*
> hangs on to the back of the cab, her
> hair in my face. A warm smell of
> wood smoke and pepper. Then dust.

Chubasco the grey sky. A *Campesino* walking in the ditch, a
    sheet of plastic around his shoulders. Tassles of rain fringe
    his sagging cowboy hat—
How I long for these people, their chickens. The fields
    and mud houses, pigs and palm thatch. Their sticks,
    their *tortillas*, their babies and thongs, machetes,
    the *leña* and *milpa*, cowboy hats, and their darkness
    after sunset.

And now they are mine—a family: *Orlando*, *Nely*, and *Jandy*,
    who is almost a year old, in the *aldea*, in the dark.

Why am I suddenly so incompetent? Why am
I always the one to go sliding down the
mountainside in a cloud of dirt? The one to
grab the bean stalk growing in a hill full of
biting ants? The one to fill his shirt and shorts
with ticks while digging *yucca* roots? The one
to chop the spiney vines so they snap back in
his face?

Orlando and I outside brushing our teeth.
Stars. Thousands and thousands and thousands and thousands.
"How is it" says *Orlando* "that the satellites can drive
        for years on the sky without crashing
        into all those stars and planets? How do they do it?"
I want to say there just aren't as many stars
        for *norte-americanos*.

How I desire these people, this village. I am
        sick with the love of them with cough, parasites,
        have not shit all week.
And always the children find me squatting hopelessly in the fields,
        my pale skin shining like a signal flare:
        "*¡Ahi está el gringito!*" "*¡Hola, chele!*"

I am torn from a dream in which men and
women wander through High Park Zoo carrying
small children in colourful baby packs, pointing
at burros and peacocks through a chicken-wire
fence—by a rooster landing on my toe.
Explosion of mutual shock. Koko-rico. Kaboom.
Shower of feathers.

"¿What can we feed to the *gringo*?
He won't eat his *tortillas* any more
and even the fried beans don't
entice him. He is almost as thin as
Orlando already and if he dies I am
sure they will excommunicate us at
least!"

O the endless *tortillas*.
(What is a *tortilla*?
A breakfast food. A lunch food. A
    supper food.
A piece of beige rubber. Warm. Damp.
Stiff velveeta cheese.
        Organic silly putty.
With eggs it tastes like eggs.
With dirt it tastes like dirt.
With beans it still tastes like dirt.
A culinary anti-climax.
Comestible disappointment.

Tortilla and *tortilla* and *tortilla*,
Creep at this petty pace from day to day.)

                Today the moon rose early and sat
                in the doorway over the orange trees.
                Nely was showing it to *Jandy*:
                "*La luna la luna la luna la luna*" she sang.

Crowds of children follow me everywhere in my village
"as if he were *Jesus Cristo*" say the parents.
Asking for songs. French songs.
English songs. "*Que reste-t-il de nos amours.*"
"Leavin' on a Jet Plane."

                Still sick. They take me to a dark hut
                and rub pig fat on my stomach and
                rub and knead and make me drink
                water with English Salts and walk
                directly to Sonaguera where the priest
                has a toilet and I can spend all day
                sitting on it and read *La Ciudad de
                Alegría* where a guy goes and lives
                with the poor and eats their food and
                gets their diseases in Calcutta. And
                just loves it.

That night I have two wet dreams about *Nely*
    in the spare bedroom of the rectory.
No change of underwear of course.
On the way home next day
    the fence posts sprouting to life along the road.
    Green life.
In Honduras everything so damned fertile.

> A man pays me five *lempiras*
> a day to work at deforestation with
> *Orlando*. I can work at almost a
> twentieth of his speed, though I do
> cut down the coffee plants we're
> making room for.

I figure it costs the man 11 *lempiras* a day for me to work for
him. (Tomorrow maybe we'll try something else.)

> I wake up weeping, having dreamed of
> paved roads, of Honda Accords, of
> subways, bookstores, cinema, billiant
> conversation, cheesecake and apples,
> bathtubs, cablevision, woollen sweaters.

Swimming in the river today.
Twenty-five children, four adults and me neither one nor the other.
    "Keep your mouth closed in the water *gringo*."
    My heightened vision can discern the dysentery, fecal coliform
and coloured fevers floating just under the surface. I lower myself
into the warm water.

> Little crabs scuttle in the warm
> shallows and minnows dart in pools.
> The brown river is alive with laughing
> and splashing. "What is 'river' in your
> language?" "What is 'sun'?" "What is
> '*pendejo*'?" they ask. Not waiting for
> an answer.

Nely asked me tonight if she could read
one of my books, shyly. "Of course" I
said and she lit a little fire in the middle
of the floor and knelt in front of it for
three hours.

Rapt. Hardly moving.
Two hundred twenty pages.
Hair tangled around her face.
The orange flicker on her dark eyes.

In the forest *Orlando* asks me about the book.
    "It didn't really happen that way did it, the story?
    The elves that came from the moon?
    And the sasquatches?"
I distract him from these questions by flipping a leaf-full of army ants
    down my collar
    and then sitting down next to a coral snake.
"The *gringo* knows most things" *Orlando* has told his mother,
"but he *is* clumsy."

And then I am the one who flies to the moon
    or at least to El Progreso,
    Coca-Cola, Teem and electric lights.
At the *Colegio San José* no chickens
    interrupt siesta.
I watch "*La Dama de la Rosa*" on T.V.

On the street I see a child in a shirt. A blue shirt.
    Colour.
The glorious apotheosis of clothing.

A Maid in Hell

Geriatric psych-ward
a whiff of urine and applesauce
are the things. A fetid sweetness.
And the air
          air
                    laundry on the dark evening
and the narrow eternity of being indoors.
Things forgotten. Old acquaintances.

> Truly among the bedpans, puréed food
> and feces, among the benzodiazepines,
> the trilafon, the chlorpromazine,
> tending to our scattered thoughts,
> tending.

If I could only.
If you could only.
If we could only.

> Leaves on the maple tree red as Pauline's
> eyes as she peers at me out of the
> shrivelled confines of her bed. The sun
> white on her wrinkled skin. She tries to
> lift her head, smooth her white hair.
> Makes apologetic sounds. Every day I
> come here to tell her stories—plots of
> operas, warped fairy-tales, the intrigues
> of non-existent politicians. Soon she is
> back asleep.

> In the distance I hear Ursula screaming.

This little world.
The locked door of this little world.
The handrail on the walls.
The tiles blue and grey and blue and grey.
The rolling lounge chairs.

Activity room. A circle of rolling chairs against the walls.
Streaming winter sun.
Closed eyes. Open eyes—
a dignified expression, a wise expression—
One face a mask of near surprise,
another frozen the instant before sneezing.
Some faces fixed at the apex of a yawn
others on the border of a sneer.

In the centre three wizened women nod together at a table.
Four others shuffle distractedly in a corner.

Snow today.
Trees are faint beyond the window.
I stare into the whiteness and
I feel Celia's chin on my shoulder.
"A stitch in time," I tell her,
"Saves nine," she replies and strides away.

If I could only.

Nurse Susan is five months pregnant
in her pink uniform. Searching for the
bad smell. Her head bobs into the lap
of each sphinx in turn. "It's Robert,"
she chirps and Robert, the left bottom
corner of his mouth wrenching
downwards, is wheeled to the
showers.

Here is Ursula, her head tilted to one side as
if she is listening to something the rest of us
can't hear. The echo of haldol footsteps
across her auditory cortex. But she never
mentions voices. "It was black, black, when
I was a girl," she says, stroking her hair, "a
little dark gypsy." She leans forward and
puts her hand on my knee. "So fresh." She
coos, "so fresh and clean young man so . . .
and so . . . and a little dark gypsy . . ."

Where are you Ursula?

Yvonne in her white uniform.
Introducing new volunteers.

> "Alzheimer patients usually go through a hostile or violent phase but most of the patients on this ward are finished with that. They aren't angry anymore because they aren't aware enough anymore. But something we do might be getting through to them. We just don't know."

The young man nudges his companion and whispers,
"It's like walking into the 'Thriller' video," he whispers.

> Icicles drip from the nostrils of the window. Grey spring tries to squeeze between starched window-frames. Mrs. Hoffman shrinks together to cough, her head ricocheting from the back of her recliner. A tongue of phlegm uncoils from her mouth. "Oh Mrs. Hoffman," sings Nurse Judy, and wipes it away.

If I could only.

> Feeding time:
> "You no good . . . ugly . . . god-damn . . . no good!" sputters Cheryl furiously. She plops her face into her dessert bowl. "Mmmmm." Grunting, she tries to pour pudding into her mouth. Spits. "You bastards. You slut. You no good. You just mind your own god-damn . . . pudding." She pulls up her blouse and wipes her face on it, exposes breasts angrily.

If you could only.

"Why don't they let us go home!" says Ursula. "Or kill me! We could go away somewhere we could just go away somewhere. We have so much money. Why don't they just kill me! I'd rather die! Why won't you let me go!" Her head tilts more and more toward the ground. "We have so much money. Kill me. My neck. My neck nick neck nick neck. Kill me. We could just . . ."

I am trying to make soothing sounds. There are no leaves on the tree outside and a sparrow hops from branch to branch.

If we could only.

Ronald is propped up in front of the television set, his face bent to the left. Three women in fluorescent tights are doing aerobics. He hammers his head stiffly on the headrest, raises his arm and hides behind it. "He likes to look at the girls," says Nurse Susan.

If they could only.

Ursula is in restraints today. "Here!" she cries, "come here!" reaching at the hurrying nurses. "Come here!"

I rush across to her.
"I am here." I tell her.
"Come here!" she screams.
"But I'm here."
"Come here *here*!" she cries, clawing at the air. I let her grab my arm. "Make love. Make love!" she howls.
"I *am* here." I repeat.

"I'm not ugly," says Ursula, "I mean not
ugly. Maybe not a great beauty. But
not ugly.
So why do they do this to me?
          A nice face. Why to me?"

          Silence seeps from the radiators over the ward
          after nightfall. The Muzak is off and sleep has
          wandered out of the patients to inhabit the
          corners of the lounge. I lead Ursula into her room.
          "Time for bed now," I say. She stands and waits.

          "Yes we'll go to bed now," she says. "It's been so
          long." She pulls her pants down but can't get her
          diaper off. "I'm so glad you're back," she says, "I
          was getting so horny."
          Cheryl groans in the next bed.
          I see our reflection in the dark window. Ursula,
          old woman, uncooperative patient, staring down
          a tired psychiatric assistant. Clearest of all is the
          glaring fluorescence above us.
          "I'll get your pyjamas," I tell her.

Advertisement on a morning game-show
for adult diapers.
The morning like the face of an old woman, sitting motionless.
I touch that face so it will know I am there;
so soft it is I can barely feel the contact.
Wrinkles soft as water.
Her toothless mouth opens.
A voice, protesting,
"But I've never seen it before, before!"

But you have. We all have.

Absent Friends

Elegy for My Friend Carol

This Sunday past
I climbed a mountain to play
horn calls up from the top
down into a green valley. Sunday it was,
in September and the September wind chilled my hands
on the cold brass. Hikers miles below looked up
at the sooty rock speckled with new snow
and the grey hard mountain light that fluttered down,
and at the howling sound I made

and in particular the black rock pile
flecked with snow that I was standing on,
and the mountain flat grey sky
reminded me of a mound of dirt
dug for your grave
while I stood there
beside your casket in the February snow
some years ago, blowing frustrated cold
horn calls inside,
and I am concerned, concerned
that the mountains and this shadowy rock seem
now to have forgotten all about you
and that I may too.

> You gave me half of your Peanut Buster Parfait
> on the school bus coming back from County
> Honour Band, since the peanuts were salted.
> "Salted peanuts in ice-cream," you protested,
> "A scandal!"

Your face that seemed always to
appear. At windows, or peering out of the O's
of your letters. Your self-caricaturing
bemused posed positioned face. Painted on

a helium balloon. Among the others.
A bright bright yo-yo. From your
highschool graduation class photo.

Winter, and when I rounded the blue mainstreet
corner, puffed with pride at the originality of the
red popsicle alternating between my chilled
hands, my boots crunched in the snow, and in the
light of the hardware-store-display window you
appeared, sudden space debris of my acquisitive
but normally leak-proof fantasy life. "Fancy
meeting you here," you said and the popsicle
broke apart in my grasp, a blushing and stunted
desperation freeze-dried instantly to the sidewalk.

And we were young it seems
and how you tortured me, then. And sat
in the grass and you were a ballerina
(you said without evidence) and
someone stuffed grass down your shirt
and we were all little dolls of fleshy light beside the school.
And I am concerned, concerned
that the grass, winter streets and red popsicles now
seem all to have forgotten you
and that I will too.

You were sitting opposite me in the school library.
Very serious. Or angry. You looked angry maybe
at me and do not look at me this way I am afraid
and I looked around and beside and behind me to
avoid your eyes and shook and you have seen this
terror act and yes I am a good actor perfect and
your mask snapped and it was all a game.

O shepherds, weep for my friend
since I never could. Pastor of Faith Lutheran
Church of Calgary. Or of Valhalla Lutheran
in Valhalla.
Come, shepherds of your intubated
flocks, your disincarnated ideals,
your ministrated doses of tradition.

Your hidebound redundant exhortations, your
misapprehension of revelation,
your prating timorous condescension,
mourn one who knew what it was
you were meant to be talking about,
for I am concerned, concerned
that the faith and the god whom she was devoted to
now seem already to have forgotten her
and I may too.

It is Thursday and the perfumed tweed of
your volubility scrapes my senses. Your
sportjacket is the evening and you and I will
speak, an ambiguous proving ground where
unpredictable angels in bucolic punk
snowsuits Volkswagen-pack our interactions,
your flushed pale extra-terrestrial eyes
transmitting mysterious intimations. We are
going to Grande Prairie Regional College
Band rehearsal, together, driven by the band
teacher. I am seventeen. The world is large.
You are its axis.

You were wearing a tan-coloured hat
and we spoke with our heads stuck out
of the eighth floor apartment's adjacent
windows. You were back from Bible
College. "Now I can just be a ballet
dancer," you said, as you always did, "a
dancer." You removed your hat and

threw it behind you. And years later, in
the cave down the hill from Sulphur
Mountain Hot Pool, with the shallow
snow falling and the steam rising, "I will
be a composer" you said, "performing
just makes you neurotic." And then
when you were suddenly an actress, in
the summer cabin heat of your place on
85th Avenue (now condos) and the light
like motor oil in the leafsmelling mornings.

And I am sorry maybe you couldn't see me
find out about your death in the rectory
of Morazán, and hitchhike over the green
Honduran mountains in a 1971 Toyota
on a stack of wood beside a pail of fish,
not knowing if I would ever get to San Pédro to
fly through the United States on sold-out airlines
and reach right up to the middle
of the Alberta February with no winter coat
to have one last look
at your mangled body in your onetime wedding dress
and verify that you were really truly and awfully dead, the way
climbing always leads to winter and graves and music and
I am concerned, concerned
that the airplanes and mountain passes and 1971 Toyotas now
all seem to have forgotten all about you
and that I may too.

On the Birth of Katherine Anne Martin

I called out to the long kitchen shadows stretching
    around behind the refrigerator, say,
    listen to this! Knock
off your Mr Fantastic routine, the
    world is changed, let's dance the *macareña*
    in Javanese, on the cupboards, I

threw open the windows to the
cold night—the stars were fixed, dilated,
    mesmerized, I
cried out—let's have a wink, or at least a twinkle
    down on the brand new child's cradle,
    or whatever they're calling the hospital version!

Downstairs I ran and told the brown spider
    on her web (and she sends
    her heartiest congratulations,
    having 730 thousand of her own) and the myriad
    dustmites too finite to fathom an event
    of such magnitude (not their fault, so am I).

My furnace and water-heater flames seemed
    flickeringly pleased at the news, swaying
    in their twin vestal chambers. Which

brings me, I guess, to my own response, which I
    can't for the life of me put into words.
    So I'll just light all the candles in the house
    and get more quick things
    dancing at the news.

Max's Bath

The dark stairway listing
under the fan of shadows cast
by its picket fence guardrail,
and you are splashing
happily, among the red and blue toys
the plastic balls and boats,

                                    for the day is
winding down and the rare spring rain and hallway
lie just beyond our
ball of light. I am
sitting on the toilet lid by the yellow-painted
water pipes, Peg leaning over the tiles of tubside
and with the steamy smell of soap and clean towels,
the newly peeled-off sagging diaper lying
limp on the tilted floor you seem
ready almost to forgive me for
having been there
while your mother was away.

You look at me and gurgle, baffling,
flavourful non-words.

What happens next? Well I hold you
while Peg gets a diaper, you yell
when she heads down the hall.
        And then you pee on me, my
shirt, a consecration
no one else has received. I hold you close,
like the cold spring rain
peering in at us, tapping the
blue windowpane with its
tiny dark and pudgy hands.

Going to a Movie (*The Bruce Lee Story*) with Lynn

Thick sandstone drapery
    of an idle summer evening, hill
        with grove of trees where
I am sitting
    pine sap glues the orange needles
on my canvas hiking pants.

And should I toss
    an idle pinecone
        out into the fading street
to wake her from her passing trance—

sure, she says, and off we go
down to that ticket taker's
    pale green door awash in foyer,
to his loud insistent voice, insisting that we enter, see
    Bruce Lee
and she who hasn't even eaten, in the popcorn lineup
    giggling and elbowing me

and while the movie runs she asks me "what's
    a *beatnik?*"—
eating corn pops two by two and
held between two fingers (daintily) precariously propped
her bare legs sprawl
upon the backs of the seats in front,
the bluish shadows flickering
along the down inside her thighs:
        O St. di Prima, Saint Jack Kerouac—
        when I saw her on the night of 1 July
        her hair a haze of comet trails;
        the golden moon, its granny glasses
        blinded, caged in clouds rimmed black
        before a field of summer grasses
        my guts were water and she a silver staircase
        twisted from those very clouds

Not that I don't know the answer—"beatnik: (*slang*)
(BEAT+nik, by analogy with sputnik.) On a morning

misted roof
rail lined with gulls and,
hush of summer memory
childhood all over the world." The salt that
stings her lips, and
unpopped kernels rattling are
whispering to me.
"Shhhhh," they're saying
"watch the movie." (Bruce Lee.)

Illustrated Advertisement for *Jerry's Barber Shop,* 77th Street, 1992

If you were to come this way,
Taking the route you would be likely to take—
If you were to come in the afternoon,
A Saturday afternoon along a street filled with people
    shopping, or looking into windows.
If you were to come below the street, where the painted pipes run
    along the ceiling.
Along the long hallway, like a man bald and retired, a man
    smoking cigarettes out of a white cigarette box, a man with a
    gentle cough.
If you were to come this way in winter, with the round snowflakes
    crowding from the sky, the sky leaning closer, over the
    storefronts
And if you were to come through the inner door at the end of the
    corridor, ajar, with a lock like the one on your bathroom, into
    the light of a bare lightbulb and a distant radio from years
    ago;
You would be in *Jerry's Barber Shop.*

> Music is playing from another time as you take your
> chair, a man in a white jacket attends to a patient,
> semi-conscious, supine in a large mechanical chair. He
> is infinitely careful, methodical, concentrated,
> monitoring pulse and respiration with breaks to wipe
> his nose. Smoke hangs in the flickering light above his
> head, while a tiny audience watches from beneath the
> paintings of sailing ships (clippers!) leaning out at
> vague angles from the walls.

A wooden coat stand takes your coat
and beckons you
toward upholstered chairs.
Inaudibility of distant voices. Jars
of liquid, filled with metal combs,
menthol unctions. A bubbling lump
of greying foam dissolves
into a porcelain oyster shell. A box of
clipper heads. The sea.

A pheromone found in human underarm sweat has
been found effective in the treatment of several types
of depression, evoking the olfactory environment
of a breast-feeding infant. This pheromone hangs
about Jerry in high concentrations, centring at the
client's face level. This place is the still centre, the
smell of church incense pastel underarm around
Jerry's white alb. It casts its glow of tranquility
about the operation. You are safe here.

And if the street outside were life outside
    you would be beneath it, amid
    the red and bluish veins of Jerry's
    barber pole, pulsing through eternity.
If the street outside were time outside
    you would be outside it, in a river
    twisting deep beneath the solid surface,
    carried along murkily in the sediment of history.
And if the street outside were you outside
    you would be behind it, your shadow, fallen
    through the earth, to blend with the shadow
    of all those surface things, the snow-strewn street,
    the voices, the buying and selling.

Jerry talks about the big trade, Messier for Nicholls, Esposito
for Ratelle, Mahovlich for Ullman. An invisible wind rattles
the pages of magazines strewn across end tables. Out of a
black void a typeface demands "Is God Dead?" A calendar
girl fades in and out, her bikini changing shape along with her
body. *Time Magazine* with embroidered borders. *The Star
Weekly. Playboy's* bunny ears. Jerry's voice coaxes the scene
into black and white. He is the nucleus of a living cell, the
smoky cytoplasm of this structure radiating outward from the
core of his actions. On weekends he cuts hair at a nursing
home. His unshaven face twisted in concentration.

And you would leave again, this subterranean
    placenta of eternity, *Jerry's Barber Shop.*
Remember this name as you blink in the sunlight—*Jerry's,* with
    prices from yesteryear, who turns back time,
    through a life
            retold in haircuts.

Preparatory Exercises for Valentine's Day

Recollected Reflection on Valentine's Day

Drip.

Drip.
Filmy darkness adheres to the shadows of my
room, cracks invisibly against the underside of my
eyelids.

Spring. It must be Spring, since waves of airborne
hormones are executing tumbling routines across
the surface of my electric blanket. Tickling softly.

And two trees have grown together above my roof, a vegetable
penthouse apartment. Their trunks twist, creak like cheap
bedsprings.

Furtive, the stiff long fingers and damp nipples
stroked bunched together in dark buds of wet.
And transpire through tongues of leaf-wriggle and
lap in soft fluids, and semi-solid the matter of
lower abdomen writhes and parting the leaf-lips
by her green clitoris and laps and veins of green
engorged the concave branches and suck of skin
and sucking sound of strange sternal fricatives.
Veined erectile shaft of his submerged penis
emergent in seed-pods sliding and flush of shivers,
a ripple pressed into agony of foreignness, slime-
shaped while showering saliva trails on stiff
slippery and smooth. The sticky mucosa sugar
slides. Slime of tangle, of twist of pubic stain
follicles the bark of tongue textures and fungal
holly scents slick in cells and cells of sperm and
coats the fibrous insides of them all.

Voices felt against a gurgle depth and surprise of strange
strained delicacy. The indescribable curves of her arched
inverted pelvis. Vibrant compression. A silky cord adheres
to branches forked and spread. As they part against the
night sky roots probe tremulously into the blue jeans of
earth.

I turn on the light, read
The Secret Life of Plants.

Valentine #9 (Phone)

In the damp electron darkness that separates us I can feel the
  muscles of your tongue glistening across the ripples of
  your laughing voice.
I am invaded, my skin quivering hungrily across my swollen chest,
  my sternum a vortex, straining to draw you toward me
  through these wires.
I feel my lips against your ear, a translucent plastic shell of blood,
  alive in its rubbery leaf-rim, hot with desperation.
Is your nose inquisitive? The polymorphous permeability of your
  voice sends a single sine wave the length of my spine, a
  reactive transmission of your sonic movement, allowing
  me vicariously to inhale
the hollows of your shoulderblades, a sartorial twitch as you shift
  from one foot to the other, and the crass fingers of your
  polyester uniform drumming nervously upon the echo
  chamber of your lower abdomen
where my disincarnate libido reverberates.

Valentine for You to Pass on to Your Sister

Does her smile still cause flippered creatures to spontaneously beach
        themselves and flop around uttering desperate cries until they
        expire from sheer pantyhose?
Does a tropical rainforest full of exotic fruits and insects still swirl in
        movement of her pelvis, in the bends of her tights, in the coral
        snakes of her shoulderblades?
Remind her I am still using only the top quarter of my lungs to breathe
        until she comes to me.

Valentine #7

The location has me confused.
I feel it all takes place out of doors and
    in a narrow street without traffic ever
        and few street-lamps. Very very flushed and clumsy and
           shaking while I breathe. Murmurs.
And here we are adults, speaking.
She
    offers me tea.

    A kiss of midnight ash, falling.
    Breathless stars, smeared over the sky.
    Polyps of whispers burst on the snow.

Valentine #11

The air clings to your body, hums with sudden tropical storms, a trembling of dewy nocturnal summer. In the valleys of your shoulderblades the atmosphere bonds preferentially to my blood, starving my capillaries with skin hunger.

I want to be lost in the vines of your neck, the ropey tissues of your collarbone. Your deltoid muscle a ripe fruit, soft with a juice I long to drink.

Mantis-like you confront me, your waist a lithe licorice pipe in black stretched lycra. I am drawn inward by meso-cyclones playing across your lips, your cheeks, glued to the space between us.

You have become a live cell among the dust phantoms of my imagination, an ecstatic cancer on my thoughts, joyously malignant.

Valentine #17

Puffing of a toy steam engine under the covers, the hillock of
 hidden bellows on the shadow moor.

The exhalations of your skin, the soil, veined with roots of
 dandelions along your ribs.

Your liquid shape absorbing me in darkness—the warm lake of
 your belly lapping against my encircling arm.

Slow depletion of oxygen in the hollow between our two noses,
 chill air in the interstices of our unit.

My penis throbbing in the valley between your buttocks, dissolving
 as I and you disappear into sleep.

Valentine #15

I push in on the door
and you pull in on the door
    wool light, night
    carriage in vitrine, red
    sweater (or possibly "sweater
    of reeds") nostrils of breeze.

O the cuisante sensation!

All the street tilted and ran into our
bald and perpendicular hearts, under its
elevated ceiling.

I can feel the candles flickering
all across the sky
while in the shadows of the parkèd cars, commerce
    continues its relentless quantification of the dark.

Bats honeycomb the air
precipitated from the receding dusk
while the ubiquitous but unseen
    flying squirrel hunts
    insects, concealed in the scotoma of the night.

Klein's Paint's neon sign is already quenched
on the expiring street;
the living room looms.
Photons of domesticity
stream from your eyes,
wrap themselves around me,
draw me inside.

Fluff is the Enemy
of Music

Translation of Richard Dehmel's *Verklärte Nacht*, framed by Schoenberg

There is something threatening
in the directness of our language.
The glowering violoncello voice,
the grainy croak in its depths, fitfully,
the damp Vienna streetcars, long sentences utilizing
obscure verb tenses, like a memory of something
once modern, now
saved from mustiness by an unchallengeable
dignity, even here. They, the performers,
are not as certain—tired, hurried, they
fidget slightly, wondering.
"When in doubt, emote," they resolve. And

yet,

it is still possible to be absolutely sincere.

The absolute exists. God exists.

The world is a picture of your hopes.

Everywhere you look there are angels.

The small lizard in the sink scampers away.

Awakening I found three small blisters on the tips of my fingers.

"Blessedness."
"Redemption."
"Purity." These words have meaning.

Sweetness. The dust descending in the window light.

It is midafternoon, summer. The sun setting outside.

The two cellos sway
like two reeds in one wind.

Seen from the perspective of the moon
              who never breathes
the blue leaves a vibrating field of
                  overlapping fractal topographies.
How can the world,
            the evening,
                  be so still?
We are walking.

"I can see so far this night—the trees the fields,
                  the sky inside me.
I am closed. Everything chokes inside
but I am absolutely certain."

All six performers for a moment synchronized like puppets on a
single set of strings.

Is it that the depth of life has become unbearable?
The pull of the heart, the sheer materiality of the world.
That in rigor (*vitis!*) a channel can be fabricated, temporarily
drawn out, diverted, worked to exhaustion,
a life inside you not your own, lyric
artifice, the cliché rubbed raw has been
coaxed into expression,

gestures the essence of nostalgia, shameless,
laughable, perfect.

A Noonhour Piano Recital in which Catherine Donkin in her Woollen Sweater plays Débussy's *Les sons et les parfums tournant dans l'air du soir*

The hesitant insinuation of water drops crawling on the window
    is the sound and
sometimes unsteady
    a single blush-trace
        flushed
on her cheek, toward her lips it
flows and ebbs;
      her fingers pulse—

> properly handled the piano can be one of the most subtle of woodwind instruments, effortlessly appropriating the sonic properties of the oboe, clarinet, willow whistle or marsh wren. Among its 88 groups of reeds tiny children drift in wicker baskets, gurgling in their sleep as miniature ducks tow them toward the listener.
>
> Its body ninety-five percent water.
>
> Its feathers made of light.
>
> The piano's lifespan usually ranges between one and sixty minutes; this afternoon's performance will witness several of these, each originating in the discarded exoskeleton of its recent ancestors. The wire and ebony abstraction we see is not then really present. It is a synesthetic artifact of her artistic vision—the material shadow thereof.

Quatuor pour la fin du temps, Banff Centre, 1994

Roubakine Hall, its basketball hoops,
and stacking chairs
spread row on row,
is fading in the summer
                    afternoon while
A chord.

                In the sky a
                bird hops
                        from sphere to
                                sphere
                mechanical bird in two dimensional celestial
                perched
                        briefly on each planet disk
                                        descending.

                It is day and yet the engines of the sky—
                Saturn, Jupiter, the moon, the map's legend—
                are visible against the matte grey sky,
                copper orbs, embossed, iconic,
                                slightly tarnished,
                and the bird,
                reedy like a
                clarinet filled with shadow
                and the sun containing
                light, lit from inside, a flat bulb
                filled with hard material radiance

The light in Roubakine watery,
dilute, weak photon solution
pooling on the floor.

                    We are sitting in a gymnasium deep beneath the Earth,
                    where it is always yesterday, the night before, a day long
                    ago when turbines hummed under the parquet floor
                    making major sevenths with the fluorescent lamp hum.

"Watching the black and white television."

"You must have fallen asleep."

"I *was* awake because I could taste the lozenge in my mouth,
        the
                trapezoid. The triangle."

"The movie was already over."

"In the screen light. On the area rug."

                "You tossed and turned, tossed and turned."

"Washing over the chesterfield, with the lake outside."

A visitor in town
through the limp summer streets—
the air settling onto sidewalks. Nothing moves.
A forgotten song plays
                inaudibly on a car radio somewhere,
the signs on the streetcorner incomprehensible: "Stop." "Wrong Way."
"Yield." "Sweat."
"Dance the *Summa Theologica*.
and make every movement conscious, explicit."

        The angel that followed me home that Christmas
        evening—
        Invisible at first, only a
        fresh pressure then
        in the headlamps of passing cars
        its little legs see-through
        as it surged ahead, running clumsily
        tripping, dragged along by its wings. Then
        again in the darkness,
        shyly, and abruptly
        fluttering into a front yard, disappearing over a
        rooftop,
        running up behind moments later, or
        peering into a secondfloor window.

Stillness is absolute in the Roubakine Auditorium, we
see, above the stage, a
hot-air balloon violinist, suspended, unmoving.
And there, above the pianobench—
furtive eyes and fingers that are minnows scattering.

> From my seat I cannot foresee the evening
> following the performance, when I will eat
> the fried and fatted calf, breaded,
> with unctuous crunching.
> I will see these four performers eating there
> oblivious.

Light settles now
in Roubakine Auditorium. An audience
brings together hands in thanksgiving, shouting,
"Bravo!"
   "Brava!"
    "Bravi!"
But not, of course,
   "Alleluia."

Free Translation of Mahler's
"*Ging Heut' Morgen übers Feld*"

The lawns are fresh and eager brushcut
pools with emerald sun
the road lies thick between them
caved and cratered, numbly
flaking—grey scales breathe
beneath my feet.

Goodmorninggoodmorninggoodmorning. Yes!

And to the left the last white row
of houses in the village stands,
its back to this year's fallow fields,

a fetid stream flows though a culvert,
splashes rotting fishhead smells
onto the road then disappears

And I look up, longing—
loose cords of steam unwind
       into the sky somewhere—
       off beyond, the
       rippling birch and linden, the fields,
       terraced in the morning haze.

Pedagogy of the Orchestral Horn

Yes from the beginning of the universe to your town
prefigured in the spiral of galactic arms
the conturnations of rotating dust,
outlines of graphed attractors,
storms, hurricanes, occluded fronts—
the double helix at the foundation of your physiognomy
to the misguided intuition of the Bohr atom
coils and coils of music, our song.

                        You
                                are the sound and I could
hear the gentle gurgling
        of the corrugated tubing, stylized loops
                and ropes, sounding
                        when I laid my ear against her belly

                                my brother, a boy then
                                waterskiing off the off
                                        the off
                                                the the
                                        the *Gewandhaus*, the house of yarn in
                                                loops and whorls, buoyant
                                water wheels
                                buoying up this boy
                                        the Orchestra
                                its long and looping rows of horns.

Buoying up the sound, a wind,
                through the door ajar—

First I will teach you:

wind—
        the candle's fingers their sweeping
like windstirred
        skeleton branches
                capillaries
                        minor
                                alterations to the Mandelbrot set
resulting
        stretching in
                harps and strings of shoes.

Fingers waxing toward from the windblown candle, strung,
    fingers their sticky pads palpating

This I will teach you:

        Nota: the first progenitor of this, this HORN
predates earthly life as such for when the LORD (and don't try to
say this for heaven's sake) YHWH appointed the great spiralling
whorl of the youthful galaxies their enormous external genitalia
undescended testicles and circle of hair on his forehead[1] (downy
blond willowy like the poplar fluff but without this creature's[2]
extension[3]) and this was on a chill December night
(windless ice by the lake front)
the circumnutation of astral arteries and
(the corpuscles passing in single file
each one (they are rolling hub caps
hoops king snakes
chased with a stick—wriggling their
shoulders along the walls as they
advance)) each strains toward these
first multicellular animated artifacts:
    1) the proto-ancestral sponges
    (whorl, whorl)
    2) the (not yet chambered)
    nautiloids.   Unplayable.
        in their (and I have to keep re-asserting this)
        spiral chitinous carapaces littering the ocean floor
        (actually a page from *Time-Life's* volume on Evolution)
like the worktable
        of Carl Geyer, Keith Berg's workshop[4] littered with
leadpipes[5] and valveslides.

---

[1] and do please forgive this extrapolation on the newborn Buddha's elephantine organs
[2] and also forgive my pronomial subsumption of the fluff into a creationist cosmology.
[3] and while you're at it, in the last footnote maybe forgive my lifting fluff out of its
phenomenal anonymity. Fluff is the enemy of music.
[4] Carl Geyer was apparently a prominent hornmaker of the twentieth century.
[5] as in "to lead" pipes, not Pb

This too in the present we will learn:
               in this studio
               where the thick wrappings
               tangled roots of pipes and poplars
               listing walls and window sills
               thick with dust and shifting—
               beyond the window's
               grey insulating membrane the sun
               soft like an orange squashed
               against the grim horizon
               gathers the grey light into itself
               as we do when we breathe.
               But while you are playing the shadows
               are luminous, alive with a glow
               of concentration.
               While you are playing the pipes are murmuring
               creeks and rivulets in the midwinter twilight
               dark between the snow[1]
               and as the printed music (Arban's "The Art of
               Phrasing") gradually merges
                         into the grey

                         pages.

---

[1]Visual reference is to "The Wood-gatherers" at the AGO by Mr. van Gogh.

Anton Bruckner: Fourth Symphony, First Movement

In the soft nightlight marking your seat number—
you hear the highway
from the cornfield's heart
    damp evenings after rain, with the mud
clumping your gumboots
    tractorroad
            curved in the gravel.

And the ephemeral assertiveness of
wind in the windrows.
Nebulous heroism in the
    bovine distant voice wishing
        high in the powerlines.
            And there is that thumping oxbrained iteration,
            pug hey-come-over-here hard-of-hearing   nose-
            blower into hand gathering like gathering darkness
            up in your fist.
Make it one thing, tied with
    repeating loops of electric fence, humming down the field,
test it with a cornleaf, throb pulse
                    pulse in your shoulder
    stare blank into the valley, road river, sound
everywhere crowding your lungs, water
    in the air material as music in the evening growing
slowly colder, and then:

stillness is upon you
before you can even see it coming.

Acknowledgements

Thanks to Don McKay, the editor of this book, and to Jan Zwicky, for editing the final section.

Thanks also to:
    Bert Almon
    Katja Davidson
    Chris Dewdney
    Tim Lilburn
    Doug McCarthy
    Clint Morril
    Notes from the Underground Writers Group
    Allan Richards
    Ann Stevenson
    Shelley Sopher

Some of these poems in different versions have appeared in *Grain*, *West Coast Line*, *Pottersfield Portfolio*, *Absinthe*, and *The Malahat Review*.

Biography

Ken Howe was born in Edmonton, moved to Beaverlodge, Alberta when he was 9, and now lives in Regina with his friendly pit bull Zuki. He has played principal horn in the Regina Symphony for eight years. Ken is a member of the Council of Canadians, the Canadian Centre for Policy Alernatives, and R. Murray Schafer's Wolf Project. Ken was the recipient of the 2000 City of Regina Writing Award. The manuscript for *Household Hints at the End of Time* received a John V. Hicks Manuscript Award, also in 2000.